Kickstart Package

WORKBOOK

KICKSTART

PACKAGE

WORKBOOK

TORBEN SØNDERGAARD

KICKSTART PACKAGE

WORKBOOK

By Torben Søndergaard

Copyright © 2021 by Torben Søndergaard

Kickstart Package Workbook / Torben Søndergaard

Paperback ISBN: 978-1-943523-96-2

ePub (iPad, Nook) ISBN: 978-1-943523-97-9

Mobi (Kindle) ISBN: 978-1-943523-98-6

PUBLISHED BY THE LAST REFORMATION
IN CONJUNCTION WITH THE LAURUS COMPANY, INC.

PUBLISHED IN THE UNITED STATES OF AMERICA

This workbook may be purchased in paperback from
www.TheLastReformation.com, www.Amazon.com,
and other retailers around the world.
Electronic versions are also available from their respective stores.

KICKSTART PACKAGE APP

Scan the QR Code below to download the app. You can view the Kickstart Package videos and see other materials and videos to help you in your disciple walk.

6

TABLE OF CONTENTS

KICKSTART

PACKAGE
WORKBOOK

Welcome to the Kickstart Package Workbook!

We are excited to invite you on this amazing journey. With this Kickstart Package, we will help you understand what it means to be a Disciple of Christ. We believe that these seven lessons can change your life forever. This simple, biblical teaching has already changed thousands of lives worldwide, and we believe that God will also use this kickstart package to change your life!

This workbook outlines all the video lessons with questions designed to help you remember the lessons and gives you something to reflect on. You will find all of the Bible verses mentioned in each lesson and we provide space to take notes.

#TLRKICKSTARTPACKAGE

DISCIPLE OF JESUS

LESSON ONE

Length of Video: 44 min. 07 sec.

Go therefore and make disciples of all the nations, baptizing them in the name of the Father and of the Son and of the Holy Spirit, teaching them to observe all things that I have commanded you; and lo, I am with you always, even to the end of the age. Amen.
Matthew 28:19 -20 NKJV

Prayer: *God, I pray that You will transform my life and show me what it means to be a true disciple of Jesus. Open my heart, so I can receive from You.*

Welcome to **Lesson One**, the first of seven lessons in this **Kickstart Package**. In this lesson, we will be looking at the Bible, the word "Christian," and the word "disciple." We are going to look at what a disciple is and how we, as disciples, can learn to walk like Christ.

THE BIBLE

NOTES

- The four Gospels (Matthew, Mark, Luke, and John) describe the time leading up to the cross.

- We don't see in the 4 Gospels how people got baptized in Jesus' name, and received the Holy Spirit before the cross and before the Holy Spirit was sent down to the earth.

- The book of Acts is the only historical book in the New Testament that shows how the early disciples got born again and followed Jesus, preaching the gospel, healing the sick, and casting out demons like we should today.

THE BIBLE
66 BOOKS

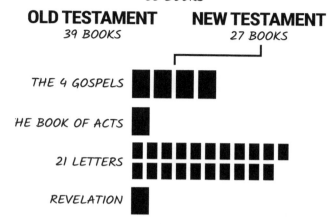

OLD TESTAMENT
39 BOOKS

NEW TESTAMENT
27 BOOKS

THE 4 GOSPELS

THE BOOK OF ACTS

21 LETTERS

REVELATION

- After the book of Acts, we have 21 letters written by Paul, John, Peter, James, and Jude. They are each writing to already born again believers dealing with church issues, theology, and much more.

- The book of Acts shows something no other book shows:
  ▸ How the early church preached the Gospel to unbelievers.
  ▸ How the early church laid hands on and healed the sick.
  ▸ How the early church cast out demons.

JESUS IS THE SAME

- Jesus is the same yesterday, today, and forever, and we can experience him the same way today.

YESTERDAY   *TODAY*   *FOREVER*

WHAT IS A DISCIPLE?

> The next day, as they went on their journey and drew near the city, Peter went up on the housetop to pray, about the sixth hour.
>
> *Acts 9:10 (NKJV)*

- Ananias is an example of a disciple like you and me. What he experienced in Acts 9, we can also experience today.

- Jesus never used the word *Christian*. He used the word *disciple*. In the Bible, you will only find *Christian* three times, but the word *disciple* you will find over 250 times.

- Today, just like Ananias, we can also experience:
  - God speaking to us
  - Being led by the Holy Spirit
  - Laying on of hands and being healed
  - Baptism in water and receiving the Holy Spirit

It's okay that we don't look exactly like Jesus now, but it's not okay that we don't look more like Jesus now than we did last year!

RELATIONSHIP OR RELIGION

- There is a big difference between Religion and Relationship. Jesus didn't come with religion but for us to have a relationship with the Father through Christ.

- True Christianity is a supernatural life with Jesus, performing miracles, and being led by the Holy Spirit in our daily life wherever we are.

> "Woe to you, scribes and Pharisees, hypocrites! For you cleanse the outside of the cup and dish, but inside they are full of extortion and self-indulgence. Blind Pharisee, first cleanse the inside of the cup and dish, that the outside of them may be clean also.
>
> *Matthew 23:25-26 (NKJV)*

- True Christianity is from the inside out.

- True Christianity is to be born again and to get to know God.

- True Christianity is an amazing life with Jesus, 24/7, led by the Holy Spirit and experiencing amazing things, like we read in the Bible.

- True Christianity is a supernatural life with Jesus, performing miracles, and being led by the Holy Spirit in our daily life wherever we are.

QUESTIONS

Reflect on what you have learned so far. You learned about the Bible and what it means to be a disciple of Christ, as described in the book of Acts.

1. How many books are in the Bible?

    a. 61

    b. 66

    c. 70

2. The book of _____ is the only historical book in the New Testament, showing how the early disciples were preaching the Gospel to unbelievers and what they did to get born again.

3. Ananias was an example of a disciple like you and me. In one day of his life, he experienced:

How _____ spoke to Him.

How he was led by the _____ _____.

How he laid hands on Paul who was _____.

How he baptized Paul in _____ and with _____.

REFLECTION QUESTIONS

1. What is the difference between the disciples described in the Bible and the Christianity that you have experienced in your life?

_____

_____

_____

_____

_____

_____

_____

2. What do you need to change in your life to be a disciple of Jesus as we read in the Bible?

_____

_____

_____

_____

_____

_____

_____

_____

_____

_____

_____

_____

_____

_____

_____

_____

_____

_____

_____

_____

_____

_____

_____

_____

_____

_____

_____

_____

_____

_____

_____

②
THE NEW BIRTH

LESSON TWO

Length of Video: 49 min. 22 sec.

Jesus answered, "Most assuredly, I say to you, unless one is born of water and the Spirit, he cannot enter the kingdom of God.
John 3:5 (NKJV)

Prayer: *God, please come with Your Holy Spirit, soften my heart, and open my eyes to understand what it means to be born again and truly following You.*

Welcome to **Lesson Two** in this **Kickstart Package**. In this lesson, we will look at what it means to be born again. This is a very important topic because we cannot live the life Jesus has called us to live as His disciples if we are not born again.

NOTES

- The normal Christian life is:
  - A life where you walk in holiness
  - A life where you preach the gospel
  - A life where you are led by the Holy Spirit
  - A life where you heal the sick and cast out demons

HOLY LIFE

PREACH THE GOSPEL

LED BY THE HOLY SPIRIT

HEAL THE SICK & CAST OUT DEMONS

> For I delivered to you first of all that which I also received: that Christ died for our sins according to the Scriptures, and that He was buried, and that He rose again the third day according to the Scriptures
>
> *1 Corinthians 15:3-4 (NKJV)*

It's NOT enough to:

You NEED to EXPERIENCE it!

- The Gospel is the good news, but it is only life-changing for those who believe it and experience it through the new birth.

> Jesus answered, "Most assuredly, I say to you, unless one is born of water and the Spirit, he cannot enter the kingdom of God."
>
> *John 3:5 (NKJV)*

It's NOT enough to:

You NEED to be BORN AGAIN!

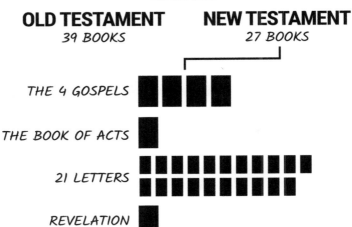

THE BIBLE
66 BOOKS

OLD TESTAMENT
39 BOOKS

NEW TESTAMENT
27 BOOKS

THE 4 GOSPELS

THE BOOK OF ACTS

21 LETTERS

REVELATION

- The book of Acts is the only book in the Bible where we see people getting born again.

WHAT SHALL WE DO?

REPENT

AND BE

BAPTIZED

*EVERYONE OF YOU,
IN THE NAME OF JESUS CHRIST
FOR THE FORGIVENESS OF YOUR SINS
AND YOU SHALL RECEIVE THE GIFT OF THE*

HOLY SPIRIT

Acts 2:37-38

THIS IS THE CROSS

Jesus died	→	We die to ourselves	→	Turn away from our sin, and turn towards God
Jesus got buried	→	We need to bury our old life	→	Be baptized to Jesus Christ
Jesus rose again	→	We need to rise with Christ	→	Receive the Holy Spirit.

THIS IS WHAT IS HAPPENING TODAY

- Sometimes people will:
  - ▸ First repent, then get baptized in water, and then receive the Holy Spirit
  - ▸ Or they first repent, then receive Holy Spirit, and then get baptized in water like we read in Acts 10 with Cornelius and his house
  - ▸ The importance is that you have to experience all three

> For I am not ashamed of the gospel of Christ, for it is the power of God to salvation for everyone who believes, for the Jew first and also for the Greek.
>
> *Romans 1:16 (NKJV)*

- Repentance has to do with acknowledging sin and with making the choice to turn away from sin

REPENTANCE
TURN AWAY

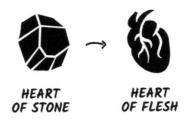

HEART OF STONE → **HEART OF FLESH**

- Also read 1 John 3:5-9.

> *Everyone who is truly born again cannot continue living willfully in sin.*

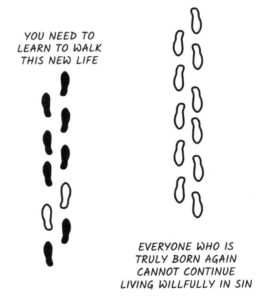

YOU NEED TO LEARN TO WALK THIS NEW LIFE

EVERYONE WHO IS TRULY BORN AGAIN CANNOT CONTINUE LIVING WILLFULLY IN SIN

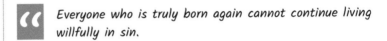

If we confess our sins, He is faithful and just to forgive us our sins and to cleanse us from all unrighteousness.

1 John 1:9 (NKJV)

BAPTIZŌ MEANS TO DIP OR TO SUBMERGE

▸ Baptism is full submersion in water for the washing away of your sins, which is activated by your faith. It is not just a symbol.

BE BAPTIZED FOR THE FORGIVENESS OF YOUR SINS
ACTS 2:38

DIE WITH CHRIST RISE UP WITH CHRIST
ROMANS 6:3-7

PUT ON CHRIST
GALATIANS 3:27

WASHING OF REGENERATION
TITUS 3:5

RISE UP AND BE BAPTIZED AND WASH AWAY YOUR SINS
ACTS 22:16

CIRCUMCISION BURIED WITH CHRIST
COLOSSIANS 2:12

BAPTISM THAT NOW SAVES YOU
1 PETER 3:21

THEY GOT BAPTIZED
RIGHT AWAY

ACTS 2   ACTS 10   ACTS 16

- Understanding Salvation in Jesus Christ through the Old Testament

Or do you not know that as many of us as were baptized into Christ Jesus were baptized into His death? Therefore we were buried with Him through baptism into death, that just as Christ was raised from the dead by the glory of the Father, even so we also should walk in newness of life. For if we have been united together in the likeness of His death, certainly we also shall be *in the likeness of His resurrection*, knowing this, that our old man was crucified with *Him*, that the body of sin might be done away with, that we should no longer be slaves of sin.
For he who has died has been freed from sin.

Romans 6:3-7 (NKJV)

- There are many today who are still slaves to sin because they:

  ▸ Haven't fully turned away from their sin with a repentant heart. *(They still have a stony heart.)*

  ▸ Were baptized before they repented and understood what baptism truly is. *(Still carry around the old body and are therefore a slave to their sins.)*

  ▸ Have not yet received the Holy Spirit and are not walking by the Holy Spirit. *(Don't have the power to live this new life.)*

QUESTIONS

Reflect on what you have learned so far. You learned what it means to be born again and walk as a disciple of Jesus. You also learned about true repentance and what baptism truly is.

1. *Finish this verse*: What shall we do to be saved?

_____ and be _____

every one of you, in the name of _____

_____ for the forgiveness of your sins

and you shall receive the gift of the _____

_____ (Acts 2:38).

2. You must be born of _____ and

_____ to enter the Kingdom of God. (John 3:5).

3. True repentance is: *(choose which ones are correct)*

   a. To pray a sinner's prayer for forgiveness

   b. Being a good person

   c. Turning away from sin with a changed heart and with hatred towards sin, just as God hates sin

4. True baptism is:

   a. An outward symbol of your inward faith

   b. A sprinkling of water when you are a baby

   c. Being submerged in water for the forgiveness of your sins, and then turning away from your sins

REFLECTION QUESTIONS

1. Am I truly free from my sins, or do I still walk like a sinner?

_____

_____

_____

_____

_____

_____

2. Have I been baptized after I repented and truly buried the old life in baptism, or do I need to be baptized again? If so, what are the sins I need to turn away from and bury in baptism?

_____

_____

_____

_____

_____

_____

NOTES

_____

_____

_____

_____

_____

_____

_____

_____

_____

_____

_____

_____

_____

_____

_____

_____

_____

_____

_____

_____

_____

_____

_____

_____

③
THE HOLY SPIRIT

LESSON THREE

Length of Video: 41 min. 38 sec.

But the Helper, the Holy Spirit, whom the Father will send in My name,
He will teach you all things, and bring to your remembrance all things
that I said to you.

John 14:26 (NKJV)

Prayer: *God, I pray that You will help me understand who the Holy Spirit is and how to to receive Him, so He can help me walk more like Christ.*

Welcome to **Lesson Three** in this **Kickstart Package**. In the last lesson, we looked at repentance and baptism in water. In this lesson, we are going to look at the baptism with the Holy Spirit and speaking in tongues.

THE PROMISE OF THE HOLY SPIRIT

- What Jesus could and could not do (John 7:37-39):
  - ☑ He could speak about the Holy Spirit
  - ☑ He could teach about the Holy Spirit
  - ☑ He could explain about the Holy Spirit
  - ☒ He could not baptize in the Holy Spirit

> Nevertheless, I tell you the truth. It is to your advantage that I go away; for if I do not go away, the Helper will not come to you; but if I depart, I will send Him to you.
>
> *John 16:7 (NKJV)*

DO NOT LEAVE JERUSALEM BUT WAIT!

- Receiving the Holy Spirit is so vital that Jesus commanded the disciples not to leave Jerusalem before first obtaining the Holy Spirit, which God our Father has promised to all who believe.

> When the Day of Pentecost had fully come, they were all with one accord in one place. And suddenly there came a sound from heaven, as of a rushing mighty wind, and it filled the whole house where they were sitting. Then there appeared to them divided tongues, as of fire, and one sat upon each of them. And they were all filled with the Holy Spirit and began to speak with other tongues, as the Spirit gave them utterance.
>
> *Acts 2:1-4 (NKJV)*

- You and I can experience this amazing life; the promise of the Holy Spirit is for everyone who believes.

FOR THE

PROMISE

IS FOR YOU
AND YOUR CHILDREN
AND FOR ALL WHO ARE FAR OFF
FOR ALL WHOM THE LORD OUR GOD WILL CALL.

HOLY SPIRIT

Acts 2:39

PROPHESIED 600 YEARS BEFORE

- Holy Spirit is the fulfillment of prophecy →Ezekiel 36:27, Joel 2:28-32, and Acts 2:16-17

- In the Bible, what happened when the early disciples received the Holy Spirit?

PHILIP
SAMARIA

▸ *IT IS NOT AUTOMATIC*
▸ *THERE IS A VISIBLE SIGN*

PETER
CORNELIUS

▸ *SPEAKING IN TONGUES*
▸ *MAGNIFYING GOD*

PAUL
EPHESUS

▸ *PAUL PLACED HIS HANDS ON THEM*
▸ *THEY SPOKE IN TONGUES AND PROPHESIED*

Acts 8:12, 15-16; Acts 10:46 and Acts 19:6

SPEAKING IN TONGUES

PHYSICAL LANGUAGE

- Speaking in tongues means speaking in a language. It can be a known language such as English, Danish, German, etc., or it can be a spiritual language like the ones we read about in the Bible.

SPIRITUAL LANGUAGE

- Three types of spiritual tongues in the Bible that:

  ▸ **BUILD UP YOURSELF:** The personal tongue is a prayer language that is between you and God. That is where you speak mysteries to God, and no one understands you. You are building up yourself, and the Holy Spirit intercedes for you (1 Corinthians 14:2-4, 14-18).

  ▸ **BUILD UP THE CHURCH:** The second tongue is to build up the Church, and this is where we need someone who can give the interpretation. One person at a time speaks aloud, and someone in the church then gives the interpretation for God to build up the church (1 Corinthians 14:27-28).

  ▸ **REACH THE WORLD:** The third tongue is to reach the world by speaking in a known language through the Holy Spirit. It is where you supernaturally speak a language unknown to you, but a language others know (Acts 2:6).

> When you are born in the natural, you learn a natural tongue that is between you and others. When you are born in the Spirit, you receive a spiritual tongue (the personal tongue that is between you and God). That is where you pray to God with your tongue, either spoken or unspoken. This tongue is for all who are born again. By living close to God, you can experience how God also lets you experience the other supernatural tongues we read about here.

HOW TO RECEIVE THE HOLY SPIRIT

> If you then, being evil, know how to give good gifts to your children, how much more will your heavenly Father give the Holy Spirit to those who ask Him!"
>
> *Luke 11:13 (NKJV)*

▸ You can pray to God and receive the Holy Spirit directly from Him.

▸ You can get others who have the Holy Spirit to lay hands on you and pray for you to receive.

NOTES

_____

_____

_____

_____

_____

_____

_____

_____

_____

_____

_____

_____

_____

_____

_____

_____

_____

_____

_____

_____

_____

_____

_____

_____

QUESTIONS

Reflect on what you have learned so far. You learned about the promise of the Holy Spirit and how you can receive the Holy Spirit. In this lesson, you also learned about speaking in tongues and the importance of it.

1. Finish this verse: Nevertheless, I tell you the truth. It is to your advantage that I go away; for if I do not go away, the _____ will not come to you; but if I depart, I will send Him to you (John 16:7).

2. Who is the promise of the Holy Spirit for?
   _____

3. What was the sign Peter saw in Cornelius's house (Acts 10) that showed him the people there had received the Holy Spirit?
   a. They went to Church every Sunday
   b. They confessed Jesus
   c. They spoke in tongues

4. The _____ tongue is a spiritual language between you and God.
   ▸ The second tongue is to _____ the church, and it needs to be interpreted.
   ▸ The third tongue is to reach _____ and does not need an interpretation because they will understand what you are saying.

REFLECTION QUESTIONS

1. Have I already received the Holy Spirit? If not, what do I need to do to receive Him?

_____

_____

_____

_____

_____

_____

2. In what area have I misunderstood the importance of speaking in tongues? What can I do to remind myself to speak in tongues more and to build myself up in my relationship with God?

_____

_____

_____

_____

_____

_____

_____

_____

_____

_____

_____

_____

_____

_____

_____

_____

_____

_____

_____

_____

_____

_____

_____

_____

_____

_____

_____

_____

_____

_____

THE GOOD NEWS

LESSON FOUR

Length of Video: 43 min.

For God so loved the world that He gave His only begotten Son, that whoever believes in Him should not perish but have everlasting life.
John 3:16 (NKJV)

Prayer: *God, thank You for Your Word. Please open my eyes so I can understand the gospel. Help me understand how sin came in and destroyed it all, but how Jesus is the answer, and how I can experience Him today.*

Welcome to **Lesson Four** of this **Kickstart Package**. In this lesson, I will use many Bible verses to share the Gospel from the beginning to the end. We will start in the book of Genesis, the first book of the Bible, and read about the Garden of Eden, how everything was perfect and how it all went wrong. We will end in Revelation, the last book of the Bible, where everything will once again be perfect, as God created it to be from the very beginning.

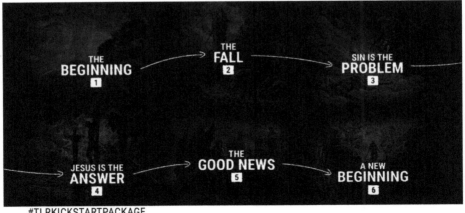

THE BEGINNING

- When God first created the earth and put man in the Garden, everything was very, very good (Genesis 1:31).
- Adam and Eve walked with God and had close fellowship with Him, like we are all called to (Genesis 2:15-17).

THE FALL

- They sinned when they disobeyed God and ate of the Tree of the Knowledge of Good and Evil, and they were thrown out of the Garden so they would not eat of the Tree of Life and live forever in their fallen, sinful state (Genesis 3:22-23).
- Sin entered into the world through the fall of Adam, and death came to all because we all have sinned (Romans 5:12).
- Sin multiplied and filled the whole earth, and God judged the world by the flood. But as soon as Noah came out of the Ark, we had a problem again because sin is not just on the earth but deep inside man (Genesis 6:5-6).

SIN IS THE PROBLEM

- Have you committed murder or adultery in your heart? (Matthew 5:21-22, 27-30)
- No one becomes righteous by keeping the law, but only by faith in Jesus Christ (Romans 3:20-22).
- If you have broken just one point of the law, you are guilty of breaking them all (James 2:10).

JESUS IS THE ANSWER

- Jesus came to save us from our sins (Matthew 1:21).

- Jesus was baptized in water, and the Holy Spirit came over Him (Matthew 3:16-17).

- He then began to preach, "Repent, for the kingdom of Heaven is at hand" (Matthew 4:17).

- He told people to repent and be born again out of water and spirit (John 3:5-7).

- He told them to deny themselves and take up their cross and follow Him (Matthew 16:24-25).

- Then He died on the cross for you and me (Matt 27:28, 31, 46, 50).

- But because He was without sin, death could not hold Him. He rose up the third day and went to heaven and sent His Holy Spirit down to us (1 Corinthians 15:1-4 and Acts 1:4).

- He is truly the Way, the Truth, and the Life, and no one comes to the Father except through Him (John 14:6).

 It costs everything to follow Jesus. We need to lay down our lives as He laid down His!

THE GOOD NEWS

- Now we need to experience how the Gospel is powerful to save us. We do that when we believe in it, as Peter says: "Repent, and get baptized in water and receive the Holy Spirit" (Romans 1:16 and Acts 2:36-38).

- When you do this, God will give you a new heart, and put His Spirit inside of you (Ezekiel 36:26).

- Now you are the one, as Jesus' disciple, who will go and proclaim the good news to others, healing the sick and casting out demons (Matthew 10:7-8).

- We now need to continue in Jesus because it is the one who stands firm to the end who will be saved (Matthew 24:13-14).

A NEW BEGINNING

- Jesus will one day very soon come back and judge the world. It's up to man once to die and then to face the judgment (Hebrews 9:27-28).

- But for those of us who are in Christ, born again, washed clean from our sins, we will have access to eat of the Tree of Life and will live forever and ever (Revelation 22:14).

It's NOT enough to:

You NEED to EXPERIENCE it!

ACTION NOW

- It's your life, your decision, but we are all here to help you. Ask those around you to help you today, to pray with you and to baptize you to Christ and with the Holy Spirit. If you don't have anyone, you are welcome to contact us. You can find our contact information in the back of this workbook.

QUESTIONS

Reflect on what you have learned so far. You took a journey through the Bible from the beginning in Genesis to the New beginning where you are now. You learned about the Fall of Man and how Jesus is the answer to everything. Jesus will one day rule in a new heaven and earth where everything will be good and perfect as God meant it to be.

1. How did sin enter into the world, and why did death come to all mankind?
   _____
   _____

2. God is NOT behind all the _____ we see on the earth today, and one day, He will make everything good again.

3. It's not enough that Jesus died on the cross for me if I don't _____ it.

4. Finish this verse: Acts 2:38, "Repent, and let every one of you be baptized in the name of _____
   _____ for the remission of sins; and you shall receive the gift of the _____
   _____"

REFLECTION QUESTIONS

1. If my family and friends could see all that I have done and thought, do I think they would still say I am a good person? What then about a Holy God Who sees everything?

_____

_____

_____

_____

_____

_____

_____

2. Where am I in this journey when it comes to my salvation:

   a. Non-believer

   b. Believer, but not yet truly repented from my sins, and born again.

   c. Repented, but have not been baptized in water (after I repented) nor received the Holy Spirit.

   d. Repented, and have been baptized in water, but have not yet received the Holy Spirit.

   e. Repented and received the Holy Spirit, but, like in the house of Cornelius in Acts 10, have not yet been baptized in water.

   f. Born again (I have repented, been baptized in water, and have received the Holy Spirit).

NOTES

KNOWING GOD

Length of Video: 38 min. 40 sec.

Therefore, if anyone is in Christ, he is a new creation; old things have
passed away; behold, all things have become new.
2 Corinthians 5:17 (NKJV)

Prayer: *God, I pray that You will help me know You more and learn to hear and obey Your voice.*

Welcome to **Lesson Five** of this **Kickstart Package**. In this lesson, we will be sharing about knowing God. So far, we have talked about discipleship, the Gospel, and how to be born again. We hope that you learned and have come to faith in Jesus, repented, been baptized in water, and received the Holy Spirit. If you have done this, congratulations! You are now born again! You are a new creation. The old has gone, and something new has begun. Welcome to a new and amazing life with God.

NOTES

NEW CREATION

- Everything we do should come out of a relationship with God because we love Him and want to obey Him.

    - ✓ New Creation: Something new has started
    - ✓ New life with Jesus
    - ✓ New Job: Sent as His ambassador

 **TO WALK LIKE HIM**

 **TO TALK LIKE HIM**

 **TO BE LED BY THE HOLY SPIRIT LIKE HIM**

 **TO HEAL THE SICK CAST OUT DEMONS LIKE HIM**

> For by grace, you have been saved through faith, and that not of yourselves; it is the gift of God, not of works, lest anyone should boast. For we are His workmanship, created in Christ Jesus for good works, which God prepared beforehand that we should walk in them.
>
> *Ephesians 2:8-10 (NKJV)*

KNOWING GOD AND HEARING HIS VOICE

THE SPIRIT   THE BIBLE

- God speaks to us through His Word, the Bible, and the Holy Spirit brings it to life!

> And they said to one another, "Did not our heart burn within us while He talked with us on the road, and while He opened the Scriptures to us?
>
> *Luke 24:32 (NKJV)*

- You, too, can experience how the Holy Spirit opens up the Scriptures to you, how it burns inside of you, and how the Bible comes alive, just like we read when Jesus walked with His disciples on the road to Emmaus.

- We need both the Spirit and the Word to walk with God. We need both to learn to listen to what the Spirit of God (the Holy Spirit) is saying to us and what the Word of God (the Bible) is saying to us.

THE SPIRIT — VISIONS, DREAMS, LITTLE VOICE INSIDE OF US...

THE BIBLE — WE RENEW OUR MIND TO KNOW GOD'S WILL, WE TEST

> I beseech you therefore, brethren, by the mercies of God, that you present your bodies a living sacrifice, holy, acceptable to God, which is your reasonable service. And do not be conformed to this world, but be transformed by the renewing of your mind, that you may prove what is that good and acceptable and perfect will of God.
>
> *Romans 12:1-2 (NKJV)*

- God can speak to us with a thought or impression.
- We can check what we hear by testing it through His Word so that we can know:
  - ▸ *When it's the enemy*
  - ▸ *When it's our own thoughts*
  - ▸ *When it is God*

> *Get the Word inside of you by reading it, meditating on it, listening to it, and reflecting on it. Let the Word be part of your life.*

SHARE EVERYTHING, SPEND TIME WITH GOD

- Prayer is life; we need to share everything with God. He wants to speak to us and build up our relationship with Him.
  - ▸ It can be in a room where you kneel and pray to Him.
  - ▸ It can also be walking and talking with Him.
  - ▸ It can also be driving in your car, or at anytime or at any place.

FELLOWSHIP WITH OTHERS

FAMILY

- We also learn to walk with God by learning from other people who are farther along than we are. This is also called *discipleship*. We are not called to live this life alone.
- You are not baptized into a church or an organization, but into a family.

> I write to you, little children, because your sins are forgiven you for His name's sake. I write to you, fathers, because you have known Him who is from the beginning. I write to you, young men, because you have overcome the wicked one.
>
> *1 John 2:12-13 (NKJV)*

- There are new babies in the faith in a family, children who are a little stronger in the faith and learning to walk, and parents who are there for the young ones.
- We need each other because we don't grow up overnight; it takes time.
- Therefore, find a good fellowship to join, a place where you can learn and grow.

QUESTIONS

Reflect on what you have learned so far. You learned who you are in Jesus. You understand what it means to be born again: that you are a new creation with a new life and a call from Jesus. You also learned what it means to know God and how to hear His voice.

1. As _____ of Christ, we are to represent Him and His kingdom here on earth.

2. In what way does God communicate with us?

   a. Through His Holy Spirit

   b. Through the Word of God

   c. Through dreams, visions, and thoughts

   d. Through His family, people around us who love and obey Jesus

   e. All of the above

3. When I am born again, I am, as the Bible says, a newborn and need to _____ up. And that is why I need a _____ of believers who can help me.

4. The more I spend time with God in _____ and his _____, the more I will know Him and His will for my life.

REFLECTION QUESTIONS

1. Now that I have heard how God speaks to us, what can I do to hear His voice better?

_____

_____

_____

_____

_____

_____

2. Where am I in my spiritual walk with God (baby, child, parent)? In what areas do I need to grow in my relationship with God, and what can I do to help that happen?

_____

_____

_____

_____

_____

_____

_____

_____

_____

_____

_____

_____

_____

_____

_____

_____

_____

_____

_____

_____

_____

_____

_____

_____

_____

_____

_____

_____

_____

_____

⑥
THE CALL OF JESUS

LESSON SIX

Length of Video: 38 min. 33 sec.

Then He said to them, "Follow Me, and I will make you fishers of men.
Matthew 4:19 (NKJV)

Prayer: *God, I want to be a good and faithful servant. I pray that You will teach me and equip me to be a good worker and to see good fruit out of my life. God, here I am: send me out into the harvest.*

Welcome to **Lesson Six** of the **Kickstart Package**. We have now looked at what a disciple is, the Gospel, how you can be born again, how to know God, and how to walk by the Holy Spirit. In this lesson, we are going to look at what Jesus called us to do and how we can serve Him.

NOTES

THE CALL OF JESUS

- The call of Jesus is for everyone, not just for pastors, leaders, and those who are ordained. No, it is for you and me and all who are disciples of Jesus.
- The call of Jesus is everywhere in our everyday life. It is not only something that is happening in a church, or from a pulpit, platform, or mission field.

THE CALL OF JESUS IS FOR EVERYONE

LUKE 10

 "The harvest truly is great, but the laborers are few; therefore pray the Lord of the harvest to send out laborers into His harvest."

- The harvest is not the problem and will never be the problem→the problem is the workers! It is you and I.

- Therefore, we should pray to the Lord to send out workers to the harvest, and we should go out ourselves.

 "Go! I am sending you out like lambs among wolves."

(NKJV)

- Jesus has not promised it to be easy, but He has promised us that He will go with us when we go out. The Good Shepherd goes with the lambs. But we need to start to go.

- The first few times, we go out to talk about Jesus, offer to pray for somebody, heal the sick, cast out demons, baptize in water, and in the Holy Spirit. We often feel like a little lamb, nervous, afraid, full of doubts. When you take that first step, you will experience that Jesus, the Good Shepard, is with you!

V4 "Carry no money belt, no bag, no shoes; and greet no one on the way."

- God will provide for your needs and take care of you when you go out and do His work!

V5-6 "Whatever house you enter, first say, 'Peace be to this house. If a man of peace is there, your peace will rest on him; but if not, it will return to you."

- Whenever you go out, you are not looking for just anyone: you are looking for someone specific. You are looking for a person of peace.

- A person of peace is someone God is drawing to Himself (John 6:44). A person of peace is interested in what you have to say and wants to hear more about the Gospel and this life with Jesus.

- There are many persons of peace out there. It can be your neighbors, someone from your school, job, family, or someone out there you haven't met yet. You just need to keep looking; you will find them.

> No one can come to Me unless the Father who sent Me draws him; and I will raise him up at the last day.
>
> *John 6:44 (NKJV)*

V10-11 "But when you enter into a town and are not welcomed, go out to the streets and say, 'Even the dust of the town we wipe off of us as a warning to you...'"

YOU WILL MEET TWO KINDS OF PEOPLE

- Those who ARE NOT a person of peace: don't spend all of your time talking with them. Just move on to the next.

- Those that ARE a person of peace: take the time to share Jesus and don't be too fast to move on.

TWO EXAMPLES OF A PERSON OF PEACE

- An example of a person of peace in the Bible is Lydia from Acts 16:13-15, who welcomed Paul into her house. Lydia and the members of her household were all baptized.

WHAT MUST I DO
TO BE SAVED?

- Later in Acts 16:30, we see the jailer as another example of a person of peace. He asks Paul and Silas, "What must I do to be saved?" When people ask questions like this, it demonstrates they are interested in what you are saying. This is a big sign that they are a person of peace!

So they said, "Believe on the Lord Jesus Christ, and you will be saved, you and your household." Then they spoke the word of the Lord to him and to all who were in his house. And he took them the same hour of the night and washed their stripes. And immediately he and all his family were baptized.

Acts 16: 31-33 (NKJV)

⑥ LESSON SIX: THE CALL OF JESUS

61

START!

▸ Share the Gospel

▸ Use our resources

▸ Find person of peace

▸ Lead them to Christ

▸ Keep it simple

▸ Follow Jesus

HEAL THE SICK AND PREACH THE GOSPEL

V9 "And heal the sick there, and say to them, 'The kingdom of God has come near to you.' "

- We are called to heal the sick, cast out demons, and preach the Gospel as Jesus has called us to. You can do this! Don't be afraid to try! When you do this, you will see that Jesus is with you, and you will start to see people healed, set free, and born again.

PREACH THE GOSPEL

REJOICE THAT YOUR NAME IS WRITTEN IN HEAVEN

HEAL THE SICK CAST OUT DEMONS

IT'S OKAY

WE DON'T LOOK EXACTLY ↓

LIKE CHRIST NOW

BUT WE SHOULD

LOOK MORE LIKE HIM NOW ↓

THAN WE DID LAST YEAR

Remember: It gets easier and easier the more you do it!

I DID IT
XI X2 X5 XI0...

↗ ↘

I LEARNED
I KEPT GOING

IT BECOME
EASIER

↖ ↙

I'VE DONE
THINGS WRONG

The worst thing you can do is to do nothing; those who do nothing will not save one person's life! Those who do something make many mistakes, but they learn and become better and better and see more and more fruit.

QUESTIONS

Reflect on what you have learned so far. You learned about the call of Jesus, and how we can serve Him as His disciples. We also looked at Luke Chapter 10 and Jesus' instructions to us as His disciples to go out and make more disciples.

1. According to Jesus in Luke chapter 10, is the problem with the harvest or with the workers?

_____

_____

2. *Finish this verse:* Whatever house you enter, first say, "Peace be to this house. If a man of _____ is there, your peace will rest on him; but if not, it will return to you" (Luke 10:5-6).

3. *Finish this verse:* "When you enter a town and are welcomed, eat what is offered to you. _____

_____ _____ who are there and

tell them, '_____ _____ _____

_____ has come near to you" (Luke 10:8-9).

4. A person of peace is:

    a. Someone God is calling on and drawing to Himself.

    b. Someone that is open and ready to hear what you have to say about Jesus.

    c. Someone who doesn't want to hear about Jesus.

    d. Both a and b

REFLECTION QUESTIONS

1. Who do I know around me that may be open to hearing the message of the Gospel? Who do I know that may be open to prayer for healing and deliverance?

_____

_____

_____

_____

_____

_____

_____

2. What can I do to reach the people around me? Write down some people you think may be persons of peace, or write down some ideas about how you can start to reach out to people. Should I share the Gospel myself or take someone with me? Shall I use the tools like this Kickstart Package, the movies, or other tools out there to help me to reach them for Jesus?

_____

_____

_____

_____

_____

_____

_____

⑦
THE GOOD GROUND

LESSON SEVEN

Length of Video: 44 min. 17 sec.

But the ones that fell on the good ground are those who, having heard the word with a noble and good heart, keep it and bear fruit with patience.

Luke 8:15 (NKJV)

Prayer: *God, please help me to obey Your Word and prioritize my life so that I become the good ground that produces a lot of fruit.*

Welcome to **Lesson Seven** in this **Kickstart Package**. We hope that the Kickstart Package has been a big blessing for you thus far. We believe many of you are now ready to follow Jesus as His disciples and want to bear a lot of good fruit. We believe that this last lesson in the Kickstart Package will be a big blessing to you.

NOTES

THE PARABLE OF THE SOWER

"Listen! A farmer went out to sow his seed. As he was scattering the seed, some fell along the path, and the birds came and ate it up. Some fell on rocky places, where it did not have much soil. It sprang up quickly, because the soil was shallow. But when the sun came up, the plants were scorched, and they withered because they had no root. Other seed fell among thorns, which grew up and choked the plants, so that they did not bear grain. Still other seed fell on good soil. It came up, grew and produced a crop, some multiplying thirty, some sixty,

some a hundred times. Then Jesus said, "Whoever has ears to hear, let them hear." When he was alone, the Twelve and the others around him asked him about the parables.
(Mark 4:3-10 NIV)

THE PURPOSE OF THE PARABLE

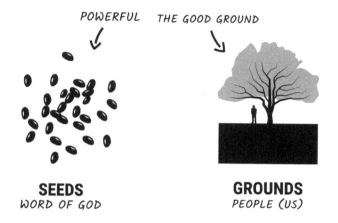

SEEDS
WORD OF GOD

GROUNDS
PEOPLE (US)

BEARING FRUIT

- Jesus wants us to bear fruit; there are two kinds of fruit:
  - ▸ There is the fruit of the Spirit → Galatians 5:22-23
  - ▸ There is the fruit where we Go OUT and bear everlasting fruit, which is souls and people? → John 15:16

FOUR GROUNDS

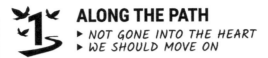

ALONG THE PATH
▶ *NOT GONE INTO THE HEART*
▶ *WE SHOULD MOVE ON*

- These are those that hear the word, but it goes in one ear and out the other. It never goes down into the ground (heart).

- Don't argue with those people; move on to the next person.

> And these are the ones by the wayside where the word is sown. When they hear, Satan comes immediately and takes away the word that was sown in their hearts.
>
> *Mark 4:15 (NKJV)*

ON THE ROCKY PLACES
▶ *DON'T HAVE DEEP ROOTS* ▶ *PERSECUTION*
▶ *FALL AWAY / COMPROMISE*

- Those who are this ground are the ones who hear the Word, and it starts to grow. Everything looks good, but when persecution comes, they fall away. If they don't fall away right away, they begin to compromise to obtain peace (Mark 4:5-6, 16-17).

- Persecution has never been the enemy of the real church. The fake believers, those who are unwilling to pay the price to follow Jesus, will fall away. The real disciples will not fall away but fall down on their knees and pray more, then see even more fruit.

> Some fell on stony ground, where it did not have much earth; and immediately it sprang up because it had no depth of earth. But when the sun was up it was scorched, and because it had no root it withered away.
>
> *Mark 4:5-6 (NKJV)*

> *You need to decide that you will NOT be ground number two and that you will keep going no matter what.*

AMONG THE THORNS
► *RECEIVE IN THE HEART BUT...*
► *WORRIES OF THIS WORLD* ► *TOO BUSY*

- Those who are this ground hear the call of Jesus and say yes to Him. They take His Word into their heart and also begin to see good fruit. But then the worries of life, deceitfulness of richness, and longing for other things come in and take the time and focus, so they don't bear much fruit.

- We need to be aware of the deceitfulness of riches, worries, and desires for other things, so that these things don't come and take our time, keeping us from bearing fruit. We need to decide that no matter what, we will put Jesus and His call first in our life.

> And they have no root in themselves, and so endure only for a time. Afterward, when tribulation or persecution arises for the word's sake, immediately they stumble. Now these are the ones sown among thorns; they are the ones who hear the word, and the cares of this world, the deceitfulness of riches, and the desires for other things entering in choke the word, and it becomes unfruitful.
>
> *Mark 4:17-19 (NKJV)*

THE GOOD GROUND
- ► BEAR A LOT OF FRUIT
- ► X30 X60 X100 TIMES

- Those who are this ground receive the Word into their hearts and don't compromise for the sake of peace. They don't let the worries of this world, the deceitfulness of riches, or a longing for other things come in and steal what God wants to do. They keep the Word, obey it, and see a lot of fruit.

- If you realize you are not this ground, ask God what you need to do to become the good ground and remain there. Start with being faithful in the small things, and God will then put you over more.

> But these are the ones sown on good ground, those who hear the word, accept it, and bear fruit: some thirtyfold, some sixty, and some a hundred."
>
> *Mark 4:20 (NKJV)*

QUESTIONS

Reflect on what you have learned so far. You learned the importance of obeying Jesus' Word and becoming the good ground that produces a lot of fruit!

1. The seed is the _____ of God.

2. People represent the four different types of _____ that the seed can fall in.

3. **Ground number 1** are those who hear the Word, but the seed goes in one _____ and out the other. It never goes down into the ground (heart).

4. **Ground number 2** are those who hear the Word, and the seed starts to grow. But when _____ comes, they fall away or begin to compromise for the sake of peace.

5. **Ground number 3** are those who hear the call of Jesus and accept the Word into their hearts. But when the _____, the deceitfulness of riches, and a longing for other things come along, they choke the Word, and it becomes unfruitful.

6. **Ground number 4** is the ground where you have received the Word into your _____, obey it, and see good fruit. It is where you don't let persecution, the _____ of this world, the deceitfulness of _____ , or any other thing come in and steal the good fruit.

#TLRKICKSTARTPACKAGE

REFLECTION QUESTIONS

1. What ground am I right now? Am I the good ground that bears a lot of fruit?

_____

_____

_____

_____

_____

_____

2. What do I need to change to become the good ground that bears a lot of fruit?

_____

_____

_____

_____

_____

_____

_____

_____

_____

_____

_____

_____

_____

_____

_____

_____

_____

_____

_____

_____

_____

_____

_____

_____

_____

_____

_____

_____

_____

ACTION PLAN

- Now that you have finished the Kickstart Package, you can put together an action plan to be sure that you end up as the good ground that bears much fruit!

- Luke 10:2, "And he said to them, the harvest is plentiful, but the laborers are few."

- Isaiah 6:8, "Also I heard the voice of the Lord, saying: 'Whom shall I send, and who will go for Us?' Then I said, 'Here am I! Send me.' "

Write down the names of people you wish to pray for, and share the Gospel or the Kickstart Package with them..

_____

_____

_____

_____

_____

_____

LESSON RESOURCES AND SCRIPTURE REFERENCES

1 DISCIPLE OF JESUS

Hebrews 13:8

Act 9:10

Acts 11:26

Matthew 17:16

Matthew 17:17

Matthew 23:25-26

Luke 6:40

John 3:3

2 THE NEW BIRTH

1 Corinthians 15:3-4

2 Corinthians 5:21

John 3:3-5

Mark 1:15

Mark 16:16

Acts 2:37-38

Acts 19:2, 5-6

Acts 10:46-47

Acts 22:16

Colossians 2:12

Colossians 3:5-10

1 John 3:5-9

1 John 1:9

Romans 1:16

Romans 6:37

Galatians 3:27

Titus 3:5

1 Peter 3:21

Acts 2:41; 16:32-33

Exodus 8-13

Romans 6:3-7, 14

3 THE HOLY SPIRIT

Ezekiel 36:26

John 7:37-39

John 16:7

Acts 2:1-4, 6

Acts 2:16-17

Acts 8:15-16

1 Corinthians 14:2-4, 8

1 Corinthians 14:27-28

4 THE GOSPEL

John 3:16

1 John 5:10-12

Genesis 1:1

Genesis 1:12-13, 18-19, 31

Genesis 2:15-17, 25

Genesis 3:9

Genesis 3:22-23

Romans 5:12

Genesis 6:5-6, 8-9

Matthew 5:21-22, 27-30

James 2:10

Ecclesiastes 7:20

Romans 3:20-23

Matthew 1:21

John 1:9

Matthew 3:16-17

Matthew 4:17, 23

John 3:6-7

Matthew 16: 24-25

Matthew 10: 34-39

Matthew 27: 28-31, 46, 50

Acts 1:4

John 14:6

Acts 2:36-38

2 Corinthians 7:10

Mark 1:15

Ezekiel 36:26

1 John 1:9

Mark 16:16

Acts 2:41

Colossians 2:21

Romans 6:3-4

Acts 8:17

Acts 19:6

Matthew 10:7-9

Matthew 24:13-14

Hebrews 9:27-28

Matthew 25:32

Revelations 22:3-5, 14

5 KNOWING GOD

2 Corinthians 5:17

2 Corinthians 5:20

Ephesians 2:8-9

Ephesians 2:10

Romans 12:1-2

1 John 2:12-13

6 THE CALL OF JESUS

Luke 10:1-11

Matthew 4:19

John 6:44

Acts 13:51

Acts 14:1

Acts 16:13-15

Acts 16:30-31

Mark 16:17-18

Luke 10:18-20

7 THE GOOD GROUND

Luke 8:15

Mark 4:38

John 15:2

Galatians 5:22-23

John 15:16

Mark 4:5-7, 15-20

Matthew 16:24, 25

Luke 10:2

Isaiah 6:8

See our free movies, online training schools, and much more.
Visit www.TheLastReformation.com

To learn more, we encourage you to go to the Online Pioneer Training School on our website,
https://thelastreformation.com/join-the-movement/online-pioneer-school/
There you will be able to complete the following 28 lessons that discuss:

1 - Come Out Of The Box

2 - Religion Or Jesus

3 - The Book of Acts

4 - Knowledge or Obedience

5 - Preach and Heal

6 - Kickstart Your Christian Life

7 - Repent, and Be baptized

8 - How to Share the Gospel

9 - Saints or Sinners

10 - Be Baptized for the Remission of Your Sins

11 - Baptism With The Holy Spirit

12 - Led By The Holy Spirit

13 - When You Fast

14 - Is God Holy or Loving, or Both?

15 - New and Old Covenant

16 - The New Covenant

17 - Reformation of the Church System

18 - Jesus' Vision for the Church

19 - Now is The Time To Do It

20 - The Reformation Has Begun

21 - Casting Out Demons

22 - Practical Lessons on Deliverance

23 - How to Understand the Bible

24 - Copy/Paste Christianity

25 - Family or Orphanage

26 - Babies, Children and Fathers

27 - Apostolic Teams: Winning Homes and Cities for Jesus

28 - Communion and IN, UP and OUT

CPSIA information can be obtained
at www.ICGtesting.com
Printed in the USA
JSHW022011080621
15705JS00003B/7